In God's Room

Marilyn Montgomery

*The Silent Presence That Speaks to Our Souls
Through Photographs, Poems, and Affirmations*

Open The Door to God's Gifts

Photographs and Poems by Marilyn Montgomery

All Rights Reserved. No part of this book may be reproduced in any form without written permission from the author.

Copyright ©2024

ISBN 979-8-9908208-1-4 (ebook)

ISBN 979-8-9908208-0-7 (hardback)

*Dedicated to
Our Creator—
The Father, Son, and The Holy Spirit*

Opening the Door to God's Gifts

God's unique creations found in all of nature are one of the most beautiful gifts found on this earth. Every variety, color, and intricate design seems to form its own purpose by awakening our spirits and touching our senses.

The beauty, design, and amazing colors along with the uniqueness come forth to light each work. The play of light and shadow creates its own pattern.

Each piece has its own message and meaning. Let them speak to you. It is as though there is a silent presence and communication that brings peace and understanding in one universal language that speaks to our hearts and souls.

See the patterns, colors, textures, and compositions that create balance, harmony, and peace in the world.

In the garden, we can connect with our God, receive His blessings, and know His everlasting presence as we view the creation of each flower and in the wholeness of nature.

It Is Here We Know God and Receive His Blessings.

Foreword

Walk through my garden and breathe in the beauty of life... as God's creations bless you in all ways.

Let the colors, textures, and designs of nature relax your mind, body, and spirit and fill your senses with renewed inspiration, joy, appreciation, and peace.

Focus on the flowers that are calling you; breathe in their color, form, and textures along with healing powers...

Listen to their messages as they affirm the goodness and peace in the life you seek...

God's Love, Beauty, and Creation open our senses and the Gateway to Our Soul with a greater understanding of our place in this world and our connection to nature.

God's

Love, Beauty, And Creation

Opens The

Gateway To the Soul

Contents

Purity 2

Light 4

Breaking Light 6

Peace 8

Angels Reign 10

Perfection 12

Springtime 14

Awesome 16

Breath Of Spring 18

Fuchsia Fusion 20

Glorious Morning 22

I Am Passionate 24

Peaceful 26

Purple Beauty 28

Heaven 30

Vibrant Light 32

Mystery 34

Blue	36
Purple Rain	38
The Glory of Morning	40
The Light Comes In	42
Morning Greetings	44
Soft But Powerful	46
Amazing	48
Cloaked In Green	50
Becoming Light	52
Pure Peace	54
Expression	56
After The Rain	58
Pink Love	60
Camelot Midday	62
Delicate	64
Light and Shadow	66
Glory	68
Grace	70
Awesome Sunshine	72
Truly Gold	74

Delicate Delight 76

Lemon Trumpet 78

Brown Eyes 80

Yellow Velvet 82

Soft Yellow 84

Orange Petals 86

Coral Delight 88

Sunburst 90

Pinwheel 92

Orange Rain Lily 94

Firecracker 96

Red Flight 98

Crimson 100

Big Red 102

Intricate 104

Magnolia In the Fall 106

Beautiful 108

Lipstick 110

Red Velvet 112

Flower Glossary 115

Enter The Gateway

Purity

There Is Holiness Within All That Is

Pure and Light

As in Christ

Bathe and Cloak

Yourself Within

This Light and Let

Purity Protect

And Free

Your Body, Mind and Soul

"Today I Am Cloaked in the Light of Purity"

Light

I Am the Light
That Shines the Brightest
Through the Darkness

My Light and Fire
Ignites Clarity
And Change

As It Burns Brightly to Heal
The Darkest Corners
Of the World

"God's Light Heals as It Radiates Out into the World"

Breaking Light

The Light in My Petals Comes
From the Heavens
As It Connects with All of Holiness

Fill Every Part of Your Essence
And All That Surrounds You
With God's Light

Feel Renewed and Aligned
Within This
The Light of Holiness

"Connect The Light of Holiness Within You"

Peace

The Silence in The Universe Is
Where the Peace and Presence of God
Resides

It Reaches Deep Within
The Hearts and Minds
Of Man and Nature

To Bring Balance and
Peace on Earth
To All Creation

"The Silence of Peace and Presence of God is Within Me"

Angels Reign

God's Holy Angels Reign
In Heaven and
On Earth

They Bring Joy, Peace and Protection
As We Call on Them
To Bless and Surround Us

We Feel Their Love As
They Embrace Us
With Their Love and Light

"God and His Holiest of Angels Reign in My Life"

Perfection

There Is Divine Perfection

In the Universe

And All of Nature

Divine Perfection

Resides

Within You

Let It

Shine Through

In All You Do

"I was Created in The Blessing of Divine Perfection"

Springtime

Springtime Ushers in New Beginnings

And the Joy

Of New Creations

As Beauty Bursts Forth

New Life and Love Presents Itself

To All of Nature

Today is a New Day

With New Beginnings

And New Light in My Life

"New Beginnings Bring New Light in My Life"

Awesome

I Am Light

And Pure

Within My Inner Core

My Strength and Connection

To God

Solidifies

As My Cloak of Purple

Surrounds

Me with Divine Protection

"God's Cloak Surrounds Me with Divine Protection"

Breath Of Spring

In The Center of My Connection
And Consciousness
I Feel Light, Airy, And Free

My Purple Edges
Contrast
The Purity of My White Petals

The Symmetry
Of My Design Brings Structure
To My Life

"I Am Light and Free When I Have Structure"

Fuchsia Fusion

From The Light

I Come Forth as A Creation

Of Beauty and Elegance

Each Of My Petals Hold

The Essence Of

Complexity and Grace

My Intricate Design

Bursts Forth to Show

The Master's Hand

"I Am Uniquely Designed by The Master's Hand"

Glorious Morning

I Greet This Morning

With Joy

As I Fully Open

My Purple Smile

Reflects A

Happy Spiritual Nature

My Design Gives Me

The Strength and Support

Needed for This Glorious Morning

"Today I Fully Open and Greet This Day with Joy"

I Am Passionate

Intricately Composed
I Am Like No Other
Flower in The Garden

My Energy Is as Vibrant
As Is My Blue and Purple
Palette

I Am

One of A Kind
Like No Other in God's Garden

"I Am One of a Kind, Like No Other"

Peaceful

Peaceful Waters
And Silence
Surround Me

Quietly I Listen
To the Stillness
In the Universe

Here Within Nature
Gently Speaks to Me
Of Higher Knowing and Wisdom

"In The Silent Stillness and Peace, I Find Inner Wisdom"

Purple Beauty

My Beauty Lies Within
Every Single Blossom
That Makes a Whole

Each One Different,
Deep Purple Contrasts
My Powdery White Outer Coat

Rising High Out of The Pond
My Flowers Reach
To Meet the Heavens

" I Am Comprised of and Supported by Wholeness "

Heaven

Let The Essence of Blue

Wash Over Your Life

Bringing Peace to Your

Heart And Soul

As God's

Power and Presence

Calms You Within

To Bring the Gift Of

The Ever Presence of Peace

"Heaven Touches Me with God's Peace and Presence"

Vibrant Light

My Blue-Purple Petals
Present A Beautiful
Watercolor Backdrop

Light Emanates from My Center
As Each Stamen
Sends Electrifying Golden Energy

Reaching Far
Feeding Hearts and Souls
With My Vibrant Energy

"Blue Vibrant Energy Feeds My Heart and Soul"

Mystery

*Mystery Waits to Be
Unveiled as Only
God Knows the Timing*

*Enter And Behold
His Wisdom That Lies
Deep Within You*

*Joyfully Receive
The Mysteries of Life
Waiting to Unfold*

"Mysteries Of My Life Unfold in Divine Time"

Blue

Express Your True Self
And Allow Your Energy To
Flow Out into The Universe

Let The World See
Your Special Light
And Individuality

Rise Up Beyond
Your Own Limitations
And Greet a New Day

"I Express My True Self and Rise Beyond My Limitations"

Purple Rain

My Petals
Reflect Both the Light and Dark
As They Become A

Delicate and Fragile Balance
Like the Shades of Color
In All of Life

Light And Dark
Is the Part of Life
That Creates Balance

"*Light and Dark Shades Create Balance in My Life*"

The Glory of Morning

There Is No Time of Day
That's More Beautiful
Other Than Early Morning

When Rays of Sunlight
Highlight My Face
To Show My Grace

It Brings Promises Of
A Beautiful New Day
Lighting My Heart and Soul

"The Glory of Sunshine Lights My Heart and Soul"

The Light Comes In

When My Colors
Come Together
The Ones Created for Me

The Light Appears
In A Moment
Bringing Amazing Clarity

The Blues and Greens
Are Surely the Colors
Chosen for Me

"The Colors I Need Appear with Amazing Clarity"

Morning Greetings

This Is a Special Morning
And I Am Here to Greet You
To Brighten Your Day

To Prepare You for Anything
That Comes Your Way
By Bringing My Calmness

Into Your Heart
To Know That
We Will Never Part

"Calmness Centers My Heart, We Will Never Part"

Soft But Powerful

My Petals Are Light in Color

My Voice Is Soft

And Quiet

If There Is a Reason

My Voice Will Speak

Out

My Stamen Amplifies

Things I Need to Say

Only in A Godly Way

"My Voice Speaks Out, In A Godly Way"

Amazing

I Become More When
I Stand In
God's Holy Light

Not Too Much Dark
Nor Too Much Light
In the Perfect Place

There
Standing with God
In His Holy Light

"With The Perfect Balance in God's Light, I Become More"

Cloaked In Green

There Are Days That I Choose

To Go Inside

To Cloak Myself

There Healing Comes In

To Rest, Restore and Protect

Me from the Outside World

When I Step Back Out

My Power and Energy

Is Stronger and Has Greater Clarity

"Rested and Restored, I Have Greater Clarity"

Becoming Light

If I Could Only Express
The Things Hidden
Deep Down Inside of Me

And Speak About
The Thoughts That Stay
Locked Inside of Me,

I Would Be as Bright
As God Light
Planned for Me

"I Allow God to Heal the Things Locked Within"

Pure Peace

My Passion for Peace,

A Gift from God

Overflows into The Universe

To Places Known and Unknown

Crossing All of Space,

Lands and Seas

Into The Hearts

Of All Mankind

God's Plan

"Peace Flows Across the Lands and Seas into My Heart"

Expression

The Past and The Present
Are Linked to The Beauty Of
My Expression

An Ole Soul
Brought into A New World
With A Knowledge of Truths

Revealed And Aligned
God's Truths Can Provide
Healing for the World

"*My Life Here Today is to Bring Healing to the World*"

After The Rain

A Touch of Rain

Feeds and Nourishes My Beauty

As It Continues Creation

Even The Rains and Storms

Are Part of The Plan

To Strengthen Me

As I Am Nourished

And Fed by The Heavens

My Life Is Led by God's Hands

" My Life is Nourished and Fed by Rains from the Heavens"

Pink Love

Graces This Pond
As It Rises from Below the Waters
To Present Itself to The World

A Background of Green Lily Pads
Contrasts the Light Pink
That Sits on Top the Water

The Golden Center Unfolds
Into a Beautiful Intricate Design
Intriguing and Mystifying Our Senses

"I Gracefully Rise and Present Myself Wholly to the World"

Camelot Midday

Beauty Infuses

The Senses

With Peace, Love, and Gentleness

My Light Pink Center

Showcases

My Outer Dark Pink Petals

In Creating

A More Magnificent

And Intricately Colored Me

"The Beauty of Nature Infuses Me with Peace and Love"

Delicate

My Delicate Form
Opens as a Gift
To Uplift Spirits

Beauty and Grace
In Simplicity Is
My Voice

My Soft Orange Inner Light
Speaks A Quiet Energy
To Highlight My Inner Beauty

"Nature, Like Me, Highlights My Inner Beauty"

Light and Shadow

God's Sunlight Accentuates
The Constancy of the Pattern
In My Petals

Large and Showy
Light and Delicate
My Essence and Statement is Bold

Beautiful and Big
Contrasting Elements Like Mine
Always Appear Very Grand

"My Energy is Bold and Beautiful"

Glory

There Is Nothing as Lovely as the
Soft Shade of Pink
Laid Upon My Petals

Droplets of Rain Fall
Creating an Electrifying Energy
That Adds Even More Beauty

My Petals Appear Very Delicate
Although I Have Great Strength
Within My Core

"Though I Appear Delicate, My Inner Core has Great Strength"

Grace

My Soft Pink Brings

Love and Relaxation

To Uplift Spirits

Each Petal with Its

Own Symmetry Creates

Order in Nature

Relaxing

Brings Focus and Clarity

To New Concepts and Ideas

"*My Clear Vibrant Energy Brings Order and New Focus*"

Awesome Sunshine

Awesome Is the Word Spoken
As My Blossom Opens
To Greet the Day

My Yellow Sunshine Center With
Pure White Edges
Is A Lovely Sight

Rain Falls Upon My Petals
Magnifying and Energizing
The Gifts from Heaven Above

"My Arms Open to Receive Gifts from Heaven"

Truly Gold

Light and Lovely
Bright and Beautiful
Bathe in My Golden Petals

Let Its Light
Shine Upon You
And Infuse Your Spirit

Connect Within
To God's Light From
Heaven to Earth

"Connecting To God's Golden Light Centers My Spirit"

Delicate Delight

Rain Feeds the Earth

And Brings Life To

My Lovely Petals

Sunlight Appears

And Washes Over Me By

Highlighting My Beauty

Pink Edges

Soften My Presence

And Show the Grace in My Face

"My Presence Brings Softness and Grace"

Lemon Trumpet

My Grand Appearance
Is Large and Loud
Graceful and Lovely

With My Trumpet Blowing
I Am One of The Most
Magnificent in The Garden

The Sunshine Amplifies
My Beauty and
Design Just for You

"I Am Magnificent"

Brown Eyes

The Palest of Yellow Petals
I Am Translucent
And Light

Veins Flow from My Tips
Only to Disappear
Into My Deep Maroon Center

A Burst of Yellow
Presents My Stamen
Beautiful, Light, and Unique

"My Design is Light, Beautiful, and Unique"

Yellow Velvet

Lovely Yellow Ruffles

In Layers

Come Together in Perfection

Rays of Sunshine

Seem to Radiate From

Each of My Petals

All to Bring Joy and Happiness

To the Garden

And to Hearts All Over the World

"Rays Of Sunshine Radiate from Within Me"

Soft Yellow

My Ruffled Petals
Come Together
To Create Great Strength

My Blooms Tightly
Formed Next To One Another
In My Family

Together
As A Unit
We Create a Whole

"We Come Together to Create a Whole"

Orange Petals

My Petals Open

To Reveal

Beauty and Creativity

My Cheerful Orange

Lifts Spirits and Stimulates

Minds and Bodies

My Energy Renews

Revitalizes

And Brings Joy to All

"My Spirit Lifts and Joyfully Revitalizes All Parts of Me"

Coral Delight

Grace, Beauty, and Intricacy
Show How Patterns in
The Universe Repeat

As My Branches Hang Down
They Showcase My Iridescent Flowers
Shimmering in The Light.

The Pinks and Oranges
Dance in and Out
As If to The Rhythm of The Sunset

"Patterns are Uniquely Created and Repeated in Life"

Sunburst

The Sunshine Reflects
Beauty, Color, and Creativity
As It Sits Upon My Blossom

A Burst of Creative Energy
Waiting to Unfold
Becomes a Part of My Life

My Color and Design
Is Carefully Painted
By God's Master Hand

"My Life is a Burst of Unfolding Creative Energy"

Pinwheel

Variance In the Shades
Of My Petals
Are A Lovely Blend

My Subtle Changes
Create
An Ebb and Flow Within

Like A Pinwheel
I Wait for The Winds
To Blow and Activate Depths of My Soul

"I Embrace Variance in Every Part of My Life"

Orange Rain Lily

After the Rain
My Beauty Burst's Forth
Heralding A New Day

Yesterday Washes Away
While Emerging New Life
Paves My Way

A Surprising Design
That Is Superior And
Unique to All

"I Am Unique"

Firecracker

My Stunning Design

Is Different

And Unlike Others

Deep Orange Blossoms

Burst Out

As If to Greet the Sun

Others Open

Slowly

One by One

"*My Messages Come One by One*"

Red Flight

A Phenomena of Nature

I Glide

Through the Skies

Playful and Illusive

My Nature As I

Glisten and Fly

Here One Moment

Gone the Next

I Am Free

"My Creative Spirit Soars When I am Free"

Crimson

My Petals Open
To Reveal
The Power of Passion

A Burst of Bold Red Energy
Projects Outward
In a Bouquet of Stamens

My Intricate Center Symbolizes Amazing
Creativity in Its
Most Beautiful and Exquisite Form

"The Power of Passion Opens and Overflows Within Me"

Big Red

There Is a Dynamic Energy
In the Intensity
Of My Red Color

It Is Filled with The Power
Needed To
Begin Anew

Activate The Energy
And Open a New Door
Within Your Soul

"I Am Infused with the Energy and Power to Move Forward"

Intricate

Like Is an Eternal Circle

Just as My Petals Dance

Around and Around

Perfectly Created

And Set in Place

My Own Exotic Design

I Am One of The Most Intricate

Of All of God's Creations

Among the Garden Faces

"I Acknowledge My Own Beauty and Unique Intricacies"

Magnolia In the Fall

Beginning as a Seed

In the Divine Plan Of

Creation and Nature

Nurtured By The

Heavens and Earth

Molded by The Winds and Rains

There, in Constant Change,

My Seeds Bloom To

Reach Their Full Potential

"I Welcome the Changes to Reach My Full Potential"

Beautiful

Oh, What Beauty
A Garden Brings
As It Feeds the Heart and Soul

It Is the Gift We Receive When
We See, Feel, and Smell
The Beauty of the Red Rose

Breathe in the Essence
And You Will Forever Know
Why the Famous Red Rose

"Breathe in the Beauty and Fragrance of the Red Rose"

Lipstick

One Of The

Softest Petals Of

The Golden Light Is Mine

My Edges Touched

By the Brush

And Light of God's Hand

I Am His With

Pink and Gold Highlights

Beautiful Just as I Am

"I Am Beautiful Just as I Am"

Red Velvet

Feel My Softness and Beauty
As I Am the Lovely
Red Velvet Rose

Touch My Petals As
Memories Awaken
From Deep Within

To The Times Before
When I Opened the Door
Touching Your Heart and Soul

"Memories Are Activated in My Heart and Soul"

God's Gifts are the World's Blessings

Flower Glossary

After the Rain: Makanani Plumeria 59

Amazing: Light Pink Calla Lily 49

Angels Reign: White Angel Trumpet 11

Awesome: Double Purple/White Datura 17

Awesome Sunshine: White and Yellow Plumeria 73

Beautiful: Red Rose Valentine 109

Becoming Light: Curcumin Mango Ginger 53

Big Red: Red Hawaiian Hibiscus 103

Blue: Thunbergia Sky Blue Flower 37

Breaking Light: White Gladiolus 7

Breathe of Spring: Ranunculus 19

Brown Eyes: Okra 81

Camelot Midday: Camelot DoubleRose 63

Cloaked in Green: Philodendron Blossom 51

Coral Delight: Thailand Orange Ice 89

Crimson: Red Passionflower, Coccinea, Lady Margaret 101

Delicate: Slaughter Pink Plumeria 65

Delicate Delight: Pinwheel Plumeria 77

Expression: Purple Moon Rose 57

Firecracker: Pride of Barbados 97

Fuchsia Fusion: Giant White and Purple Fuchsia 21

Glorious Morning: Purple Morning Glory 23

Glory: Hibiscus 69

Grace: Pink Water Lily 71

Heaven: Blue Petunia 31

I Am Passionate: Purple Passionflower 25

Intricate: Double Red Gerber Daisy 105

Lemon Trumpet: Angel Trumpet 79

Light: White Plumeria 5

Light and Shadow: Flare Rose Mallow Hibiscus 67

Lipstick: Bi-color Rose 111

Magnolia in the Fall: Magnolia Seed Pod 107

Morning Greetings: Pale Blue Bearded Iris 45

Mystery: Blue/Purple Thunbergia 35

Orange Petals: Fragrant Cloud Rose 87

Orange Rain Lily: Guernsey Lily 95

Peace: Double White Datura 9

Peaceful: Egyptian Lotus Waterlily 27

Perfection: White Phalaenopsis Orchid 13

Pink Love: Pink Waterlily 61

Pinwheel: Kimo, Rainbow Plumeria 93

Pure Peace: White Rose 55

Purity: White Elephant Hibiscus 3

Purple Beauty: Powdery Thalia 29

Purple Rain: Iris 39

Red Flight: Skimmer Dragonfly 99

Red Velvet: Red Velvet Rose 113

Soft But Powerful: Light Green Lily 47

Soft Yellow: Shell Plumeria 85

Springtime: White Pudica Plumeria 15

Sunburst: Fancy Tropical Hibiscus 91

The Glory of Morning: Blue Morning Glory 41

The Light Comes In: White and Blue Walking Iris 43

Truly Gold: Golden Ranunculus 75

Vibrant Light: Blue Beauty Waterlily 33

Yellow Velvet: Double Ruffles Hibiscus 83

Marilyn Montgomery is an avid gardener, flower photographer, designer, and writer. Her love of nature, colors, patterns, textures, and form resonates in all her works.

Here she brings the gift of her garden to life for others to enjoy and receive the same peace, serenity, and joy she finds in the presence of God's creations.

Through her photography, she reveals the detail, design, color, and form she sees. Patterns of nature run through all that God has created and bring peace and healing to those who appreciate and understand the complexities within each element, design, and creation.

Her studies through the years have also included extensive design and healing modalities. In this book, she observes how the colors, their shades, vibrations, and intensities work to change one's attitudes and emotions while transforming to create uplifting and healing qualities.

As nature speaks to her, she allows it to speak to us and provide the joy, beauty, love, and peace that God's essence places in our hearts and souls through them. Breathe in their essence and let God's presence fill your life…and through you those lives around you.

www.ingramcontent.com/pod-product-compliance
Lightning Source LLC
Chambersburg PA
CBHW051514110526
44582CB00007B/122